A SERIES OF *Drownings*

SECOND EDITION

by

Genevieve Rysik

Dear Reader,

    First and foremost, thank you for buying my book. You have no idea how much this means to me and how grateful I am to be able to share these poems with people. That said, if you are reading these poems and they resonate, I am so sorry for whatever you've been through for that to be true. I hope that this book will reach all of the parts of you that can relate as a sign that you are not alone. Remember, there can be no light without a little darkness, but things do get better.

Love,

Genevieve

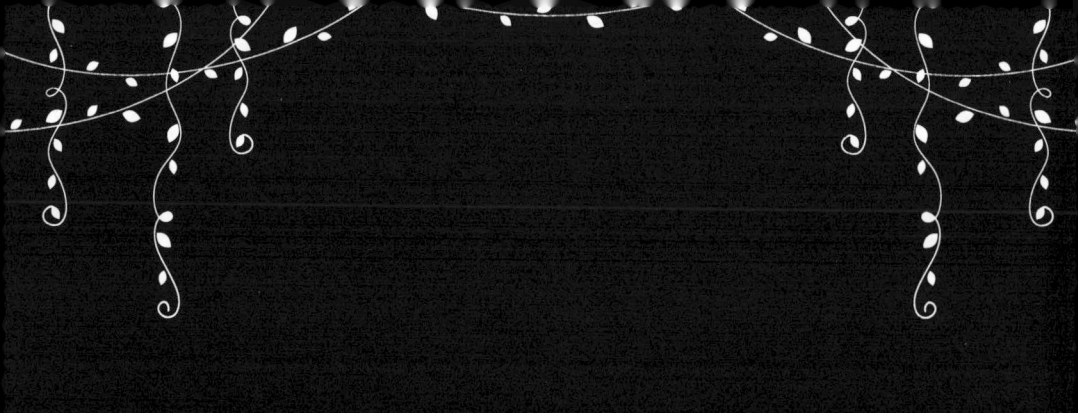

This book of poems is dedicated to my inner child.
May you find healing and peace.

Genevieve

What For?

So, you wanted to be a mother...
What on earth for?
Your own mother was no mother,
yet you chose to walk this road.
Did you ask yourself if you were healed enough?
Did you ask yourself if you were kind enough?
Did it ever occur to you-
that a baby eventually becomes a full-grown person?
Babies are not dolls
that one acquires for dress-up purposes.
I was innocent in all of this.
I deserved to be considered.
Instead, I was put in the arms of a woman
 who could not nurture,
for she herself was never nurtured.

Hurt people hurt people.
It was never personal.

Hollow

You're always saying that If things were different-

You would be somewhere else.

And that's okay because things could be different,

But you're still here.

Your self-imposed misery doesn't mean a thing to me.

If things are so awful, then please-

feel free to get your things and leave.

You make me feel hollow.

You

You were supposed to protect me.
I looked to you for comfort.
I looked to you for safety.
I looked to you...

The way you touched me wasn't safe.
Nor was the way you looked at me,
like a starved animal.
You are no longer safe.
I cannot look to you.

I do not know this version of you.
You blame me for tempting you.
But I was a child,
and you were a grown man.

You are a liar and manipulator.
You are the worst kind of opportunist.
You do not have my forgiveness.
And I will never forget what you did.

You deserved better, my darling.
You deserved more.

What You Mean To Me

You lied to me.
Manipulated me.

You say-
Not to sully your name.
But what else am I supposed to say-
When I'm asked what you mean to me?

You're a thief.
And I'll never get back what you stole from me.

You say-
Not to look at you that way.
But what else did you expect from me-
When it's all so wrong?

I trusted you-
Only to be left feeling used.

I love you.
But in the same breath, I hate you too.

Their selfishness and callous disregard for your mental and emotional wellbeing is not a poor reflection of you.

Monster

You like being the one to make me cry.
You rejoiced in my sorrow.
You're the reason I feel hollow.

You tried to siphon away my spirit.
All my light, you tried to kill it.
But all you did was dim it.

And now I'm angry and bitter,
And still wishing I was bigger,
So I can get my licks in,
Because payback's better than bitchin'

You lived in my nightmares,
Cutting off all of my air.
Deserting me in dark corners,
Always leaving me vulnerable.
Loved kicking me when I was smaller-
Just to make yourself seem taller.
A giant drunk on the power,
My own personal monster.

You don't live there in that dark place anymore.
You survived.

No Way Home

I just want you to know-
That I'm sorry if I was wrong.
As I figure out myself-
I've found I'm a little lost.

It never gets any easier,
Of that, I'm sure.
No one told me it would ever be,
But some guidance would be nice.

No one can find me here,
I'm too far gone.
I'm lost in all I fear-
With no way home.

Uncertainty is a part of life.

Show Me The Light

Look at me, my dear.
What have you done to me?
I cannot feel.
Inside, I am empty.

Stop me from poisoning my soul with spite.
Show me the light.

I cannot breathe.
Your expectations smother me.
I'm too blind to see-
Over everyone else's vision of me.

Help me since you seem to know me so well.
Show me what I'm meant to be.

F*cked Up

I'm too f-ked up for anyone to love.
Don't approach me now, or I'll just mess it up.
I'm just a sad, lonely girl,
With ugly scars etched in my soul.

I'm too messed up to make any new friends.
Get too caught up in me and see how it ends.
I'm nothing more than damaged goods.
Been poked and prodded in places no one ever should.

Meet Me In-between

Oh, won't you please give me a sign?
As I lay here with heavy things on my mind.
Won't you please dry my crying eyes?
So I can smile as brightly as the sunshine.

Oh, won't you please be here with me?
As I struggle to find the bright side.
Pick me up and help me carry on.
Lift me up and hold me in your arms.

Give me a reason to believe-
That I could be all anyone would ever need.
If I come out of hiding,
Meet me in between.

Don't Save Me

Meet me in my dreams-
In the room with wooden floors and lit candles.
Find me there on my knees-
Eyes in a cold stare, tears making rivers.

Sleeping away the pain-
Trying to escape the feeling.
Fighting every day-
Trying to make sense of my existence.

When it seems like I've lost it all,
Don't save me.
When I slip into the darkness,
Don't save me.

Don't save me.

Pretend

I'm not a little girl anymore.
I'm not a woman yet, either.
Sometimes, I don't know any better
But somehow, I do.

I walk through crowds every day.
Looking around, trying to find my way.
Like a child searching for her mom
I've never been more lost.

I don't like the way I feel these days.
The bad feelings won't go away.
Wish that I could understand.
Wish I had someone to hold my hand.

I wish I could go back and be a child again.
When I'd spin till I hit the ground again
I can't rewind my life.
Though it would sure be nice
So, I spin and play pretend.

It's Alright

I never knew that life could be cruel-
Til the day that I met you.

There you were with your deep brown eyes,
Making me weak inside.
Now, I'm trying hard not to cry-
While you turn a blind eye.

I never thought that we could be lost.
Everything we shared is gone.

Here I am now, all alone,
Breathing a heavy sigh.
Because I dodged a bullet leaving you.
Leaving you behind.

You are my past,
And I won't look back.
You hurt me bad,
But I'm alright now.

I gave you everything that I had.
All of my soul and heart in your hands.
Everything you touched turned to dust.
But it's alright now.

I Will Love Somebody...

At the time, all I wanted –
was you.
No one could've told me that-
our plans would fall through.
Now, looking back, I want to redo-
all the mistakes I made with you.
This will be my last time to
ever write a thing for you.
I will love somebody else.
They won't hurt me as bad as you have.

You didn't lose anything.
You simply let go of something that wasn't meant for you.

Train of Thoughts

In my mind
There's a train station.
I don't need a ticket-
To get where I'm going.

I'm not sure-
Where I'm going today.
There're thoughts I don't want to think about
So, I just ride away.

In my heart,
there's an empty space.
And I don't need to fill it-
To know that I'll be okay.

The train keeps moving-
At a steady pace.
And my darker thoughts-
Begin to give chase.

I fall asleep on the way-
To wherever my train of thought is taking me
My heart beats a steady beat.
As long as I'm alive,
dark thoughts will continue chasing me.

Drowning

Each day feels like I'm drowning.
No one can see me struggling.

My breaths are getting shallow-
As the water fills my lungs.

I can't breathe.
I just want to let go.

They won't help me,
I'm far beyond it.

And don't tell me-
That it's all in my head.

Pieces

When someone takes something from you
Something important that was never theirs to take,
It leaves a permanent mark on the soul.
It leaves scars in the form of unwanted memories.
Someone cut me into pieces once.
They wanted me to fit in multiple boxes.
They wanted to take each piece out and use them as they saw fit.
When someone takes something from you,
Sometimes, you can never get back what they took.

Pull those swords from your body; these sins aren't yours to atone for.

For You

Tell me where it hurts-
And I'll heal you.
You don't have to be afraid,
Because I'm here for you

I'm here for you.

He says he would never hurt you-
But he already is,
Diminishing the value of his word.
He said he'd never, but he did.

Tell me when you hurt-
And I'll free you.
You don't have to carry the pain,
Because I'll take it for you.

I'm here for you.

Tell me where it hurts.
You don't have to carry the pain.

To the little girl inside, I know it hurts right now. Know that you are loved by people far more deserving.

My Sadness

My sadness-
Is filthy sheets on a stained mattress.
It is empty bottles and cans strewn about
My sadness is cat vomit stains on the carpet.
It's piles of unread books and unused journals
It is weight gain and high blood sugar.
My sadness is photographs of past relationships.
It is rings that no longer hold meaning.
It is memories that cause more pain than closure.
My sadness is an unfinished education.
It is an undecided life path.
It is unsure steps forward while wishing to go backward.
My sadness is wishing to be alone.
It is wishing to have someone by my side.
It is years of unhealed trauma and lies swallowing me whole.
My sadness is what makes me strong.
It is what shows the world that I have survived.
It is what pushes me to move forward.

It's okay to not be okay.
This is your journey, take it one day at a time.

To Whom It May Concern

To whom it may concern,
I am tired of feeling alone.
I am tired of moving through life-
with sadness weighing on my bones.
To whom it may concern,
I want someone to care.
it's hard to listen to others' pain-
when for me, they are not there.
To whom it may concern,
my energy bank is spent.
My mind no longer allows others-
to take up space free of rent.
To whom it may concern,
I just want to be seen.
I deserve the kind of love-
that makes me feel serene.
To whom it may concern,
I will be just fine.
Many doors began to open-
as one closed behind.

Sometimes life is hard. It won't be that way forever.

Rise and Fall

Some days, I rise.
Some days, I fall.
And at the end of each day,
I find the strength to move on.

Mirror, I ask, who am I kidding?

Most days, I smile.
Although I'd rather cry.
And on better days-
I feel hollow inside.

I spend so much time-
depending on everyone else.
And at the end of the day,
I say to myself:

Who am I kidding?

If you want to go to therapy, go.
You do not need to seek permission from anyone to heal.

Crowds

I am not fond of crowds.
I get anxious and overwhelmed.
I don't know why.
I don't know where this came from.

All I know is that I am not fond of crowds.

When I was twenty-five
I tried to brave a crowded room.
I was so anxious that my face felt hot.
I wasn't breathing.

I was going to faint.
Until I wasn't.
Thank goodness for friends.
It was a work Christmas party.

I should have felt joy.
All I felt was pressure.
pressure to perform
pressure to be someone I am not

It was irrational to think
but I was sinking into my anxiety.
many tears and deep breaths later
I found myself sobbing in a stairwell

That was the day I decided
I needed to get help.
It was finally time to go to therapy.
I realized I can't do this by myself.

Don't close yourself off.
Not everyone is going to do wrong by you.

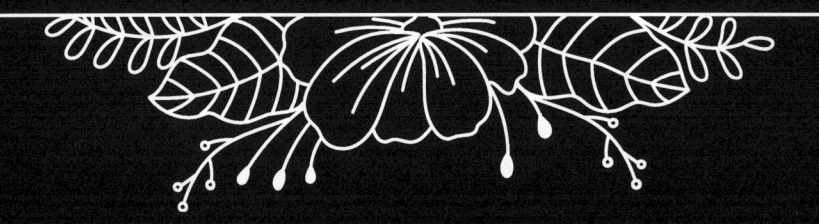

The Funny Thing About Greif

The funny thing about grief is that-
it often comes after a single or series of traumatic events.
Grief settles deep in our bones,
seeping into our bloodstream and seizing our organs.
Grief presents itself in the same manner as an illness.
Many believe that time is the ultimate healer of grief,
but that is untrue.
Time is relative,
and the passage of time does not make grief
any less painful to hold within oneself.
The funny thing about grief is that it is universal.
Grief is not exclusive to everyday occurrences such as death.
People grieve for many reasons.
Personally, my grief exists
because of the words and actions of others.
Pain does not have to be physical to qualify as painful.
Grief is uncompetitive; there is no such thing as having it worse.
As long as we are human, everybody hurts.
The funny thing about grief is that it shows up in waves.
Some days are the worst days of our lives, but others are okay.
We do not get to choose when the grief hits us.
We do not get a warning sign or a signal to help prepare us.
That's the funny thing about grief;
it is unapologetic for its presence.
It does not matter how badly we want it gone;
grief lingers like an unwelcome guest.

You are well within your right to be angry.
Apologies do not erase the things that were done or said.

Phases

You were my sun.
My earth rotated around you.
I'd do anything you wanted.
I was never my own person.

Now I'm done doing that.
I was isolated and trapped.

Your pain was magnetic.
I'd take it in like poison.
I'd let it flow through my blood—
till the darkness nearly killed me.

Now I'm done doing that.
I am gone and not coming back.

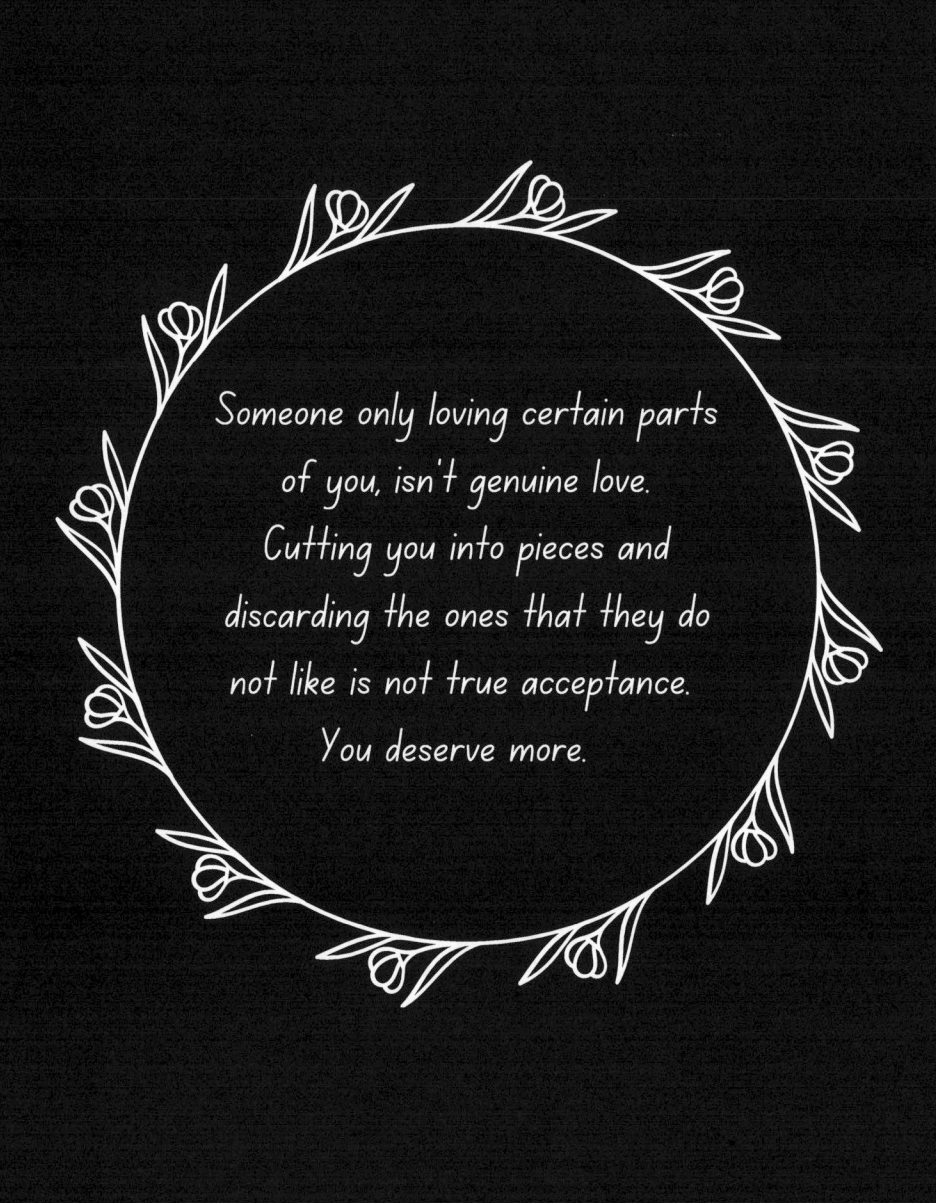

Someone only loving certain parts of you, isn't genuine love. Cutting you into pieces and discarding the ones that they do not like is not true acceptance. You deserve more.

Matter

What I feel doesn't matter.
That's what I was told.
Everything around me is set.
I have no say in what goes.

What I think doesn't matter.
That's what I've been fed.
My thoughts have no place here.
They just stay in my head.

What I want doesn't matter.
It's not about me, they said.
They know what's best for me.
As I cut myself until I bled.

I still didn't matter.

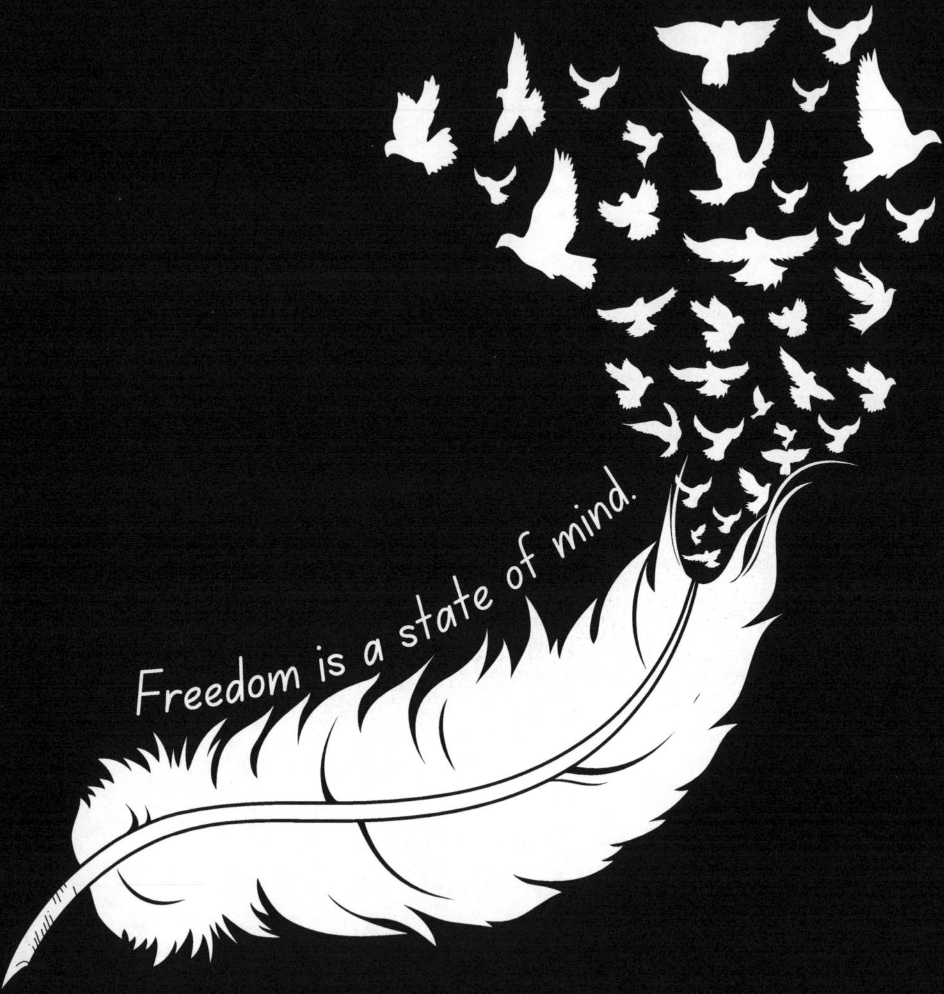
Freedom is a state of mind.

A Child's Place

Children should learn to stay in a child's place.
I used to try to do just that.
But how can a child stay a child,
When a grown man is touching her like that?

Was I only a child when it was convenient?
Until the moment you needed a fix.
When you needed your dick rubbed-
and your fingers wet,

Suddenly, I wasn't a child anymore.

Life may not be fair,
but that does not give anyone the right to make your life miserable.

Deserve

You don't deserve
for me to carry your last name.

You don't deserve
for me to forgive your wrongs.

You don't deserve
my presence in your life, or yours in mine.

You don't deserve
to know anything about me.

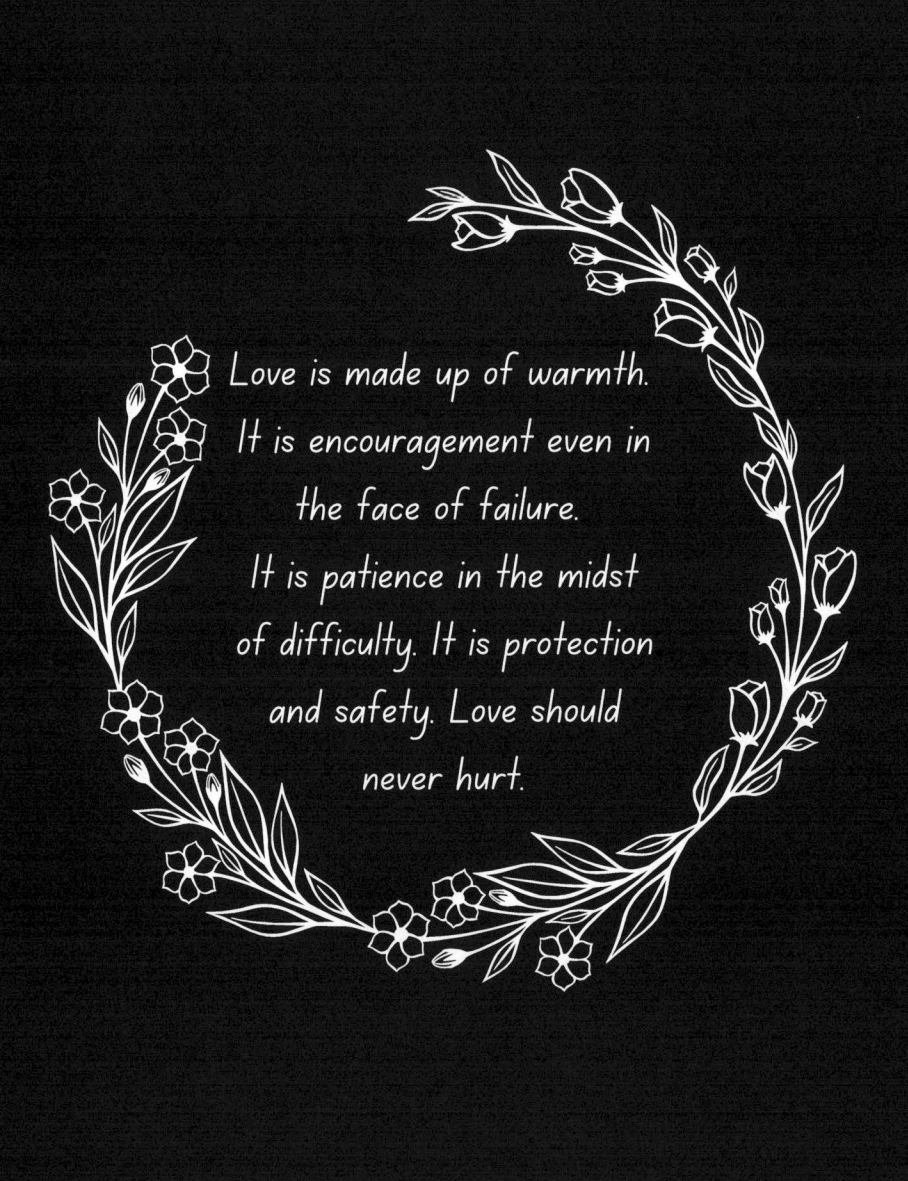

Love is made up of warmth. It is encouragement even in the face of failure. It is patience in the midst of difficulty. It is protection and safety. Love should never hurt.

Compartmentalize

Two things can be true at once.

I do love you.
I also hate you with a passion.

I do appreciate you.
I also think you are a terrible person.

I do find comfort with you.
I also want to escape from you.

I'm tired of surviving you.

Expressing your feelings is not a negative thing.

Not

I've been traumatized.
I'm not fucked up.

I've been badly hurt.
I'm not broken.

I feel righteous anger.
I'm not mean.

I feel bitterness inside.
I'm not forgiving.

In case no one has told you today,
I am so proud of you.

I Am

Though I have been hurt,
I am still kind.

Though I am in pain,
I am still loving.

Though I am still seeking,
I am open to what I find.

Though I may feel lost,
I am confident I'll be found.

Find a safe place to go and cry it out.

Sometimes

Sometimes I wonder,
why am I here?
What is my purpose?
Why have things been so hard?
Will life ever get any easier?
If words are spells,
Perhaps I've been damning myself.
Sometimes I think,
Is it all my fault?

What happened to you is not your fault.

Can't

I can't make up excuses.
I can't justify your actions.
I can't erase the memories.
I can't erase the sensations.
I can't stop feeling sick.
I can't block out the sounds.
I can't suppress my urge to flinch.
I try and try, but I just can't.

In this life, it is you vs. you.
Strive to be a better version of yourself each day.

She

Every time she screams-
I want to scream back.
But the sound is caught in my throat.
I can't make a sound, only choke.

Every time she belittles me-
I want to spit venom back.
But the words die on my tongue.
I hold it in until I am numb.

She made me question-
Whether or not I belonged.
I always felt unwanted and unloved.
Now, I can hold myself up.

Every part of you is beautiful and worth loving.

Righteous

My memories flood in piece by piece.
I see flashes of moments.
I see what was done to me and said to me.
Pieces of me being broken.

For that child, my anger is righteous.
For that girl, my anger is just.
I see the visions of my past through a cloudy gaze.
I see it is you I can never again trust.

You will grow past the pain.

Surrender

It doesn't take much to break someone's faith.
I learned very young not to believe.
It only took a series of awful events to kill it.
I have spent years trying to reclaim it.

Parts of me are still closed off and locked up tight.
I keep trying to pry myself open.
Nothing has seemed strong enough to crack my shell.
I try and try to open myself up to no avail.

This is me coming forward with open hands to say,
I surrender at your feet.
I surrender. Empty me.
I don't want to be closed off anymore.

You do not owe anyone anything,
especially not those who hurt you.

Weight

I'm failing to understand-
 the issue at hand.
What's wrong with who I am?
When you claim to love me...

I've fought for so long-
to become this strong.
Your problems are your own.
They've got nothing to do with me.

You must be so weary-
carrying envy and fury.
It must be so tiring.
Maybe you just need to let it go.

I refuse to take your hate.
I refuse to take that weight.

It must be so stifling-
The assumptions and judgments you carry.
Your baggage looks heavy.
Perhaps it's time that you let them go
I refuse to take your hate.
I refuse to take that weight.

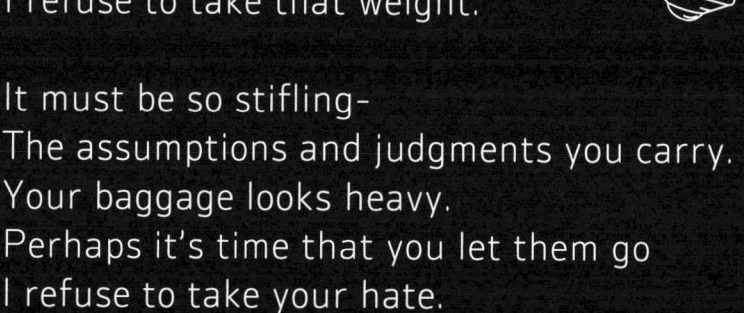

Everything is going to be okay.

Acknowledgments

I want to thank everyone who has supported me and encouraged me to publish this book.

Thank you to my best friend, Dezi, for listening to me ramble on about my dreams and encouraging me to go after them, however small they seem.

To my friend Maria, thank you for inspiring me to publish my poetry.

To my therapists, thank you for encouraging me to lean into my passion for expressing myself through writing.

Made in the USA
Columbia, SC
14 January 2025

7895352e-6cbc-4d86-b113-a700b0874b62R01